Midwinter

Zinnie Harris's plays include the multi-award-winning
Further than the Furthest Thing, produced by the National
Theatre/Tron Theatre in 2000 (1999 Peggy Ramsay
Playwriting Award, 2001 John Whiting Award, Edinburgh
Festival Fringe First award); *Nightingale and Chase*
(Royal Court Theatre, 2001); *By Many Wounds*
(Hampstead Theatre, 1999); and *Silver Whale Fish* and
Master of the House (BBC Radio Four). She was recently
awarded an Arts Foundation Fellowship for playwriting.
Zinnie Harris was Writer in Residence at the RSC,
2000–2001.

ZINNIE HARRIS

Midwinter

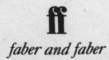

faber and faber

First published in 2004
by Faber and Faber Limited
3 Queen Square London WC1N 3AU

Typeset by Country Setting, Kingsdown, Kent CT14 8ES
Printed in England by Mackays of Chatham plc, Chatham, Kent

A CIP record for this book
is available from the British Library

ISBN 0–571–22626–4

2 4 6 8 10 9 7 5 3 1

Midwinter was first performed by the Royal Shakespeare Company in the Swan Theatre, Stratford-upon-Avon, on 5 October 2004, as part of the company's 2004 New Work Festival. The cast was as follows:

Maud Ruth Gemmell
Leonard John Normington
Sirin Jean-Claude Thompson / Jonathan Magro
Trent Sean Hannaway
Grenville Pal Aron

Director Zinnie Harris
Designer Tom Piper
Lighting Designer Wayne Dowdeswell
Sound Tim Oliver
Music John Harris
Fights Terry King
Assistant Director Emma Stuart
Production Manager Simon Ash

Characters

Maud
a woman in her thirties

Leonard
an old man

Sirin
a boy of about eight

Trent
a pedlar

Grenville
a soldier, just returned from the war

MIDWINTER

SCENE ONE

A dead horse. A woman.

The woman drags the horse on to the centre of the stage.

She takes out a large sharpened stone and starts to hack at the horse's flesh.

She hears a noise.

She stands up.

Maud Who's there?

No answer.

She returns to the horse.

Another noise.

She stands up again.

Answer me.

She holds the sharpened stone out.

I can see you.

She looks about in both directions.

One move and you've had it. I'm armed. I'm a good shot.

An old man (Leonard) and a boy appear. Leonard walks with a stick.

Leonard We smelled the meat.

Maud Don't move.

Leonard takes a step forward.

Leonard Couldn't smell anything else for miles. Half the city will be following us.

Maud It's mine.

Leonard sits down.

Leonard We know.

He signals for the child to sit down. The child sits.

The woman stares at them.

Well, eat it then.

Maud I found it.

Leonard We know.

Maud I dragged it halfway over the field. I risked my life for it.
It's mine.

She starts to eat. Ravenously.

Leonard stands up.

What are you doing?

Leonard Nothing.

She carries on eating.

Standing. Breathing. Looking at the moon.
(*to the child*) Look. Look at the moon. No need for your alarm. I'm showing my grandson the moon.

Maud That isn't the moon.

Leonard Eat your meat.

Maud It isn't the moon, that's the sun, that is.

Leonard Of course it's the moon.

Maud It's the winter sun. It looks like the moon, but it tricks you.

*She speaks with her mouth full, the horse's blood
streaming down her chin.*

Leonard Whatever you say.

Maud The moon isn't red.

Leonard Neither is the sun.

Leonard lifts the boy up. They start to move off.

Maud Where are you going now?

Leonard Back. We smelled the meat. We came. We saw
you. We saw the half-moon half-sun. And now we are
going.

Maud I'm going to have to kill you, aren't I?

Leonard We don't mean you any harm.

Maud But think about it, you've seen the meat. My
meat. You could tell someone. You could tell the town.

Leonard They will smell it themselves.

Maud Don't leave.

Leonard The boy is starving. Can't you see that? Look at
his toes pinched into the ground. His hands, his arms.

Maud We're all starving.

Leonard You have a horse.

Beat.

Maud I had a child once. But then it grew. Not very big.
But big enough to give him a gun or a knife or a set of
arrows. Big enough to sink his nails into another man's
eyes. So they said. Don't leave.

She picks up the stone.

Stay where you are.

Leonard We can't. The smell of the meat will start to make us retch.

Maud How hungry do you have to be, do you think, to eat a whole animal? In one go? The head, the eyes, the belly, the penis?

Leonard It will make you sick. Once you start you won't be able to stop.

Maud So you don't want any then?

Beat.

Tell me you'd like some. Ask me for it. Take a risk.

Beat.

Boy.

Leonard He has a name.

Maud Boy, come here.

Leonard His name is Sirin.

Maud Come here, Sirin. You'd like some, wouldn't you? You'd like some of my sick-making flesh? To fill your tummy.

Leonard Don't.

Maud Why not?

Leonard He is starving, and you are playing a cruel game.

The woman laughs.

Maud He won't starve for long. They'll decide they need him soon.

Then they'll feed him. Feed him up. Oh, there is food. Didn't you know that? We may be under siege but food does get in. After all they need food to feed the ten-year-olds they call the men.

Leonard He's eight.

Maud So they'll let him starve for another two years yet.

The woman goes back to tearing great hunks off the meat.

The boy starts playing with pebbles on the ground.

Leonard remains standing on the other side of Maud.

The woman becomes self-conscious.

She tries to carry on eating.

The boy's game becomes louder.

Eventually:

Stop that. Tell him to stop that.

Leonard What?

Maud That. What he is doing.

Leonard It's a game.

Maud I don't like it.

Leonard He is a child.

Maud I don't like it.

Leonard signals to the child to stop playing.

Pause.

Maud tries to carry on eating.

Alright. Alright. He can have some. Not you. Him.
A small piece. I'll cut it. He wants it, doesn't he? He is
a good child, sitting there playing. Not grabbing. You've
taught him well. I like his manners. I'll give him a
mouthful.

Maud cuts a tiny slither of meat and takes it to the boy.

Leonard watches carefully.

She holds it in her hand.

Come on then. You want it, don't you? Come to me.

The boy comes and eats from her palm.

He's a nice boy.

The boy grabs Maud's hand and licks the blood from her palm violently.

He then starts to try and lick the blood from along her arms and neck.

Maud pushes him away.

Leonard Careful.

Maud He was going to eat me.

Leonard You have given him a taste. What is the point in a mouthful, when he needs a meal? He will return hungrier than before.

Maud You'll find a way. You'll find something. I know men like you. You'll end up giving him your own ankles to chew.

Leonard Sirin, stand up. This woman is harmless. We should go back.

Leonard helps the boy to stand.

Maud Look at his legs. He'll be dead within the week.

The old man and the boy start to move off.

Alright. He wants a meal. I'll give him the horse. The whole thing. He can eat it bit by bit. Over weeks. Or in one go. I'll give him the horse and he'll survive. But on one condition. You give *him* to me.

Beat.

My horse for your boy.

Leonard You're mad.

Maud It's a fair swap. I gain a child and he gains a life.

Leonard What do I gain?

Maud You lose. Your part of the gaining goes to him. Don't worry, I'll look after him. I'll take over where you left off. I'll show him the moon, sorry the sun. I'll do all those things. I'll do a better job than you did.

Leonard I did fine.

Maud But you didn't get him any meat.

Beat.

Leonard I need to think.

Maud Fine. Strut around a bit. Pull your beard. Anguish. Pretend you need to make a decision. There is no decision.

Leonard Who are you?

Maud Just a woman who has a horse.

Leonard goes to the boy.

He takes the pebbles from the boy and holds his hands. Gently.

Leonard Go on then. Eat it.
The horse is yours.

The boy runs over to the horse and starts devouring.

What will you tell him?

Maud That you died.

9

Leonard He won't believe you.

Maud He'll forget you.

Leonard Yes, I suppose he will.

A noise in the bushes makes them both start.

Maud holds up the stone again.

Maud Who is there?

Leonard It'll be half the town. They'll have smelled it, I told you.
What a fool to swap a boy for a horse he must share with half the town.

Maud (*to the bushes*) Don't move. I'm armed.

Leonard It won't make a difference. They are starving. They'll storm you.

Maud I can see you. (*looking all around*) One move and you're . . .

Trent appears. He drops down onto the floor, his head protected by his hands.

He is carrying bundles.

Leonard It's a pedlar. Don't strike him. It's a pedlar.

Maud Stand up.

Trent takes his head from his arms.

Trent Two things.

Maud Stand up, I said.

Trent stands up.

Trent One: your horse is rotten, madam.

Maud Don't speak.

Trent And two: the war is over.

SCENE TWO

Maud and Sirin. They are inside a house, not a very comfortable house – maybe just a little bed at one end. It is evening, and Maud is trying to put Sirin to bed.

Maud takes a glass. Then she takes another glass.

Maud There is no milk just yet.
   I'm going to pour you a glass of water and pretend it is milk. Okay? It's a game.

   She takes the jug and pours.

Here we go. We have to pretend these things these days. We'll have milk again before long, I should think.

   She hands it out to him.

Do you like milk?

   He drinks.

And then bed. You'll like it here before long. There is a garden out the back, and a river not so far away. You might fish there like all the little boys do.

   He puts the glass back out.

   She pours more water.

What do you say?

   He drinks again.

Wouldn't you like to be able to say, more water please. Or milk, I should say, because it is milk that we are drinking after all. More milk?

   He puts out his glass.

Couldn't you say that? You could even call me Mummy if you want.

She pours water again.

And then when I pour it, thank you. That is the polite thing. Thank you, Mummy, you could say.

He drinks it again.

And he puts it out a third time.

No. No more. You'll be wetting the bed, little one.

She takes the glass away.

He snatches it back.

You can't still be thirsty.

She puts her hand out for him to give the glass to her.

No, I said.

He doesn't give it back.

Sirin, let Mummy have it?

He drops it on the floor.

Pause.

We will say that was an accident. Okay? For today that was an accident, but if you do that again tomorrow, and the next day, it won't be an accident any more.

He picks up the jug.

Put it down, Sirin. I won't tell you again.

He drinks out of the jug.

Okay, so you have had your drink now, put it back down.

He drops it on the floor, where it smashes.

There is a terrible mess.

Pause.

12

What do you want me to say? Hmm?

Do you want me to get angry with you? Do you want me to take you over my knee and thrash you?

Pause.

Sirin, please clear away the mess you have caused.

Pause.

Sirin. The dustpan is by the stove, please take it out and use it.

Pause.

I won't ask you again.

Pause.

There is a stalemate going on between woman and child.

Maud looks at the floor and makes herself busy with her hem.

The boy looks at her.

She pays him no attention.

He goes to the sink and gets out the dustpan and brush.

He gets down on his knees and sweeps.

And once you have done that you will use a cloth. There's water all over the floor.

He carries on brushing in the same place.

You have done that now, please get out a cloth.

He carries on brushing.

Sirin, you have got all the glass up.

He brushes more and more furiously.

She comes over and takes the brush off him.

You have finished now.

She takes the dustpan away and empties it.

She brings back the cloth.

He uses it on the floor.

Thank you.

He hands her the cloth back.

She stands up.

And we won't mention it again.

She puts her arms around him.

He hugs her back.

Hey!

More and more tightly.

Hey, you are going to knock me over if you aren't careful. Sirin, not so hard. Sirin?

He pushes her into the table. She catches herself. He is still hugging her.

She manages to break free.

You have to be careful.

She sits down. He comes and puts his head on her lap.

She strokes his face.

Careful, okay?

She strokes his hair.

Careful.

He starts to go to sleep.

It is going to be harder looking after you than I thought.
I had forgotten what it is like to have a boy as rough as
you. The boy I had before was not a bit like you. That is
the funny thing, you were the same age but not at all the
same. He was tall whereas you are short, he was fat
where you are thin, he was clever where you are stupid,
he was good with words, where you don't have any, he
was always helping his mother, cleaning this and that,
whereas all you do is make a mess. But you breathe,
where he does not.

How dare you breathe when he does not.

She is still stroking his head.

Hmm?

She carries him to the bed.

She puts him in it.

Goodnight, my little one. We will learn to love each other
in time.

She covers him over.

Someone knocks at the door.

Shush.

More knocking.

The boy is sleeping.

*She touches the covers then goes to look out of the
window.*

Go away.

Another knock.

I am not going to open my door to soldiers. Not tonight.
There is a boy in the house.

Grenville Open the door.

Maud I said no.

Grenville Mo, open the door.

Maud What did you call me?

Grenville Mo.

Maud That isn't my name.

Grenville Let me in.

Maud How did you know my name?

Grenville For goodness' sake, woman.

She opens the door.

She sees him.

Pause.

I tried your door earlier, but you weren't here.

Pause.

Mo?

Pause.

Maud You are supposed to be dead.

Grenville No.

Maud I was told you died.

Grenville When?

Maud Years ago. Three years ago.

Grenville They made a mistake.

Maud I got a letter.

Grenville It can't have been me.

Maud They sent your watch back, and a few other bits and pieces.

Grenville My watch?

Maud I've kept it, I'll show you.

Grenville I am no ghost.

Maud You don't look like a ghost.

Grenville I'm not.

Pause.

She reaches out to touch him.

He takes her hand.

Maud But the watch –

Grenville They made a mistake.
Here is mine, still on my wrist.

She laughs, a sort of half-laugh half-cry.

It keeps terrible time.

She hugs him.

Are you going to let me in? or are we going to stay on the doorstep all night?

She opens the door.

He walks in.

She hangs on to him.

Maud I am not going to let you go.

Grenville I'm filthy.

Maud I don't care.

Grenville I spent ten years on a battlefield.

Maud Doesn't bother me.

He kisses her.

Grenville My breath stinks.

Maud It always did.

He kisses her again.

Grenville I am not well.

Maud No?

Grenville No. My lungs, they feel like –

Maud A few weeks rest, you'll be right as rain.

Grenville Maybe.

She gets a chair.

Maud Sit down.

Grenville In a minute.

She makes him sit down.

She sits on his lap. She kisses him again.

Are you going to let me breathe?

Maud No.

She kisses him once more.

Grenville Ow.

Maud What?

Grenville You bit me.

Maud I want to eat you.

Grenville Mo . . .

He pushes her off.

She stands up.

Sorry, I . . .

He stands up.

Maud Are you here to stay?

Grenville Will you have me?

Maud Yes.

He looks around.

Grenville It's all changed.

Maud Not really.

Grenville Did you become domestic or something, this place it –

Maud It's exactly the same.

Grenville Less homely.

Maud The same.

He puts his bag down.

Grenville Who is in the bed?

Maud Isaac.

Grenville Oh
So this is . . .

Maud nods.

I never met him.

Grenville goes over and peers at him.

Sweet.

Maud He has your eyes.

Grenville Oh? My eyes.

He looks again.

Nice.

Maud They are shut.

Grenville But from the outside –

   Maud laughs.

And the rest of him?

Maud You all over.

Grenville Oh.

Maud I want to eat him sometimes, too.

   Pause.

Grenville I always imagined it was a girl.

Maud No.

Grenville Funny. I used to think about her.

Maud Him.

Grenville But in my head, her. Growing in your stomach and then, what she might have looked like the day she was born.

Maud Bloody.

Grenville But under the blood.

Maud Blue.

Grenville Then pink?

Maud Yes.

Grenville And the first time she laughed or smiled.

Maud He.

Grenville I know but –

Maud He smiled early.

Grenville Really?

Maud Clever.

Grenville Of course.

Maud And walked before his first birthday.

Grenville I'm pleased. And talked?

Pause.

Maud He doesn't talk much.

Grenville No?

Maud No.

Grenville Oh. Surprising after his mother.

Maud Maybe I talk too much, I talk for him.

Grenville Maybe.

Grenville looks over him again.

Do you think she will learn?

Maud He.

Grenville Do you think he will learn?

Maud I don't know.

Grenville He is still young.

Maud Maybe.

Grenville How old is he?

Maud Ten.

Grenville Ten?

Maud Ten.

Pause.

Why didn't you come back before?

Pause.

Grenville I tried.

Maud I don't believe you.

Grenville God knows I tried. I thought, if only I could get wounded.
  I even danced in front of the bullets.

Maud You liked fighting?

Grenville No.

Maud You must have got used to the blood and the gore, you became good at it.

Grenville You never become good at it.

Maud Maybe you preferred it to here.

Grenville Never.

Maud Maybe it's too dull here.

Grenville This is my home.

Maud You are a soldier, you're used to different things now.

Grenville I love you, that is the same.

Maud You will kill us.

Grenville Don't be stupid.

Maud You'll get angry and –

Grenville No. Never.

Pause.

He goes into his pocket.

I got you something. Nothing really, I just thought, ten years I had better bring her something.

He hands her a package.

She opens it.

Maud A ring?

Grenville It was my mother's.

Maud I remember.

Grenville I took it with me for luck.

Maud But I'm wearing it already.

Maud holds out her hand.

It came, with your watch.

Grenville looks at her hand.

Grenville That is not mine.

Maud They said you carried it around your neck.

Grenville I did. I do, but . . .
Someone else's. Maybe all soldiers carry their mothers' rings.

Maud looks at her own hand.

Maud Maybe.

Grenville Take it off.

Maud It won't budge.

Grenville Take it off.

She tries.

He tries.

Maud Oww.

Grenville I want it off. You must wear mine.

Maud You're hurting me.

23

He pulls hard.

It won't move.

He pulls again.

She yells.

It comes off.

You're too rough.

Maud rubs her finger.

Grenville Now will you wear mine?

Maud You hurt me.

Grenville I'm sorry.

She picks up the new ring.

Maud What about the old one?

Grenville Chuck it out.

Maud But I've worn it for so long I'm fond of it.

Grenville It is someone else's.

He picks it up and puts it in the fire.

Maud It won't burn, it will still be there in the morning.

Grenville Then I will take it down to the river and chuck it in. We'll never see it again.

Maud Some poor soldier died.

Grenville Lots died. Don't think about them.

He takes her hand.

Put it on, Mo.

Maud No one calls me that any more.

Grenville Maud then, put it on, Maud.

She puts the ring on.

Thank you.

He kisses her hand.

You didn't want to, did you?

Maud Of course I want to.

Grenville I forced you.

Maud No.

He looks away.

What?

Grenville Maybe I shouldn't have come.

Maud Nonsense.

Pause.

Grenville I'm not well, Maud.

Maud You have a cough.

Grenville It's more than that.

Maud How do you know?

Grenville There is some parasite that lived off us, and carried something. Lots of the men have it. I feel like . . . sometimes I can't move at all.

Maud It's exhaustion.

Grenville Or my mind, it goes out of control, I scare myself.
    My eyes water for no reason, that is the worst of it. All this stuff comes out of them, so much I can't see, and when I rub them it only gets worse.

Maud You haven't seen anyone?

Grenville Who would I see?

Maud A doctor.

Grenville Find me a doctor I will see them.

Maud It's normal, I am sure it is normal.

Pause.

Grenville And if it isn't?

Pause.

I won't ask you to nurse me. That wasn't why I came back. If it is not normal, I'll go.

He takes her hand.

I love you. I always did.

Maud I know.

Grenville Now. You can eat me.

Maud moves towards him. He laughs.

SCENE THREE

The next morning.

The bed is rumpled. Maud is alone in the house. On the table in front of her are lots of pots of earth.

She is pouring seeds into each pot.

Maud We are going to have basil, and marjoram. And parsley. I am going to make fish pie and we are going to eat it with parsley.

She pours the seeds in.

She covers them over with earth.

And lemon grass. And thyme, and if this goes well then
I will dig up the back garden and grow rhubarb. The boy
can live off rhubarb and apples.
    Apple crumble.
    With rhubarb on the side.
    After the fish pie.
    Washed down with milk.
    From the cow I will buy with the proceeds of selling
my herbs.
    And my rhubarb.

    She gets out another pot.

And in this one –

    She picks up a seed packet and reads the side.

Cinnamon
    Cinnamon?
    Can we grow cinnamon in this country?

    She looks at the side of the packet again.

If they say so. The boy will have cinnamon with his
apples and his rhubarb.
    And his milk and his pie and his apples.
    And his lemon grass.
    And his marjoram.

    Leonard comes in.

Leonard The door wasn't shut.

    She puts the trowel down.

I said the door wasn't shut.

Maud I heard you.
    Why should I shut the door? I have nothing to hide.

Leonard Where is the child?

Maud With his father.

Leonard His father is dead.

Maud No, his father is not very well, but not dead.

Leonard His other father.

Maud His father and he have gone fishing, if you must know.

Leonard How can they be fishing, there's nowhere to fish?

Maud The river is open again.

Leonard Already?

Maud The war is over. Everything is getting back to normal, didn't you know?

Leonard It's winter.

Maud You can still fish in the winter.

Leonard comes in.

There is no need to come in. You can talk from the doorway.

Leonard You remind me of my daughter – have I told you that?

Maud pays no attention, carries on putting soil into the plant pots.

You and she, it is like you learnt language from the same phrasebook.

Pause.

I want to see him.

Maud You must think I am mad.

Leonard Just for an hour.

Maud No.

Leonard It is a simple request.

Maud We did a swap.

Leonard You tricked me.

Maud It was fair as fair.

Leonard Just an hour.

Maud Not an hour, not a minute. He belongs here now.

Leonard He is my grandson.

Maud Not any more.

Leonard He is all I have got.

Pause.

Maud Then have a pot of marjoram. In fact take some basil too. You can look after them, water them, talk to them, better than a grandson, really.
Or better still, a stick of cinnamon. See if you can make it grow.

She gives him the pots. He doesn't take them.

Leonard I won't go away.

Maud Take them.

She puts them down.

We are expecting a lot of the boy.

Leonard Sirin.

Maud I know his name. Only here he is Isaac. We are expecting a lot of Isaac. His whole world has turned upside down, suddenly he has a mother and a father, a garden that he can play in, a river that he can fish in, yesterday he had nothing.

Leonard He had me.

29

Maud He needs time to settle in.

Leonard I am only talking about an hour.

Maud Later. In a week or two, when he is settled here.

Leonard Now.

Pause.

Maud Close the door on your way out.

Leonard I am not leaving. Anyway, I thought you had nothing to hide.

Maud I don't.

Pause.

Leonard Does his new father know where he came from?

Maud What?

Leonard Does his new father know where he came from?

Maud Yes.

Leonard Liar.

Maud As it happens, I took the precaution of telling him.

Leonard I don't believe you.

Maud You know nothing about me.

Leonard Then you won't mind my mentioning it to him.

Maud I will deny it.

Leonard And the horse, you will deny you stole a horse too?

Maud Anything you say. I will get you certified. Locked up. You are just an old man, no one will believe your word against mine.

Pause.

His father isn't very well, I don't want you to come in and stir up trouble.

Leonard Why should I care about that?

Pause.

Maud Why are you so poisonous?

Leonard I am only asking for an hour.

Maud And I am only asking that you leave us be.

Leonard It is an hour, not a lifetime.

Pause. Maud picks up the trowel.

Maud I've got basil, and parsley, and marjoram. We are going to have a fish pie with parsley.

Leonard I don't want to say anything. You are a good parent to the boy, I can see that. Why would I want to jeopardise that? You have the rest of your life with him, you can surely spare me an hour?

Pause.

Maud Half.

Leonard Half?

Maud Half an hour. Don't ask me for more. It is half an hour or nothing. And don't thank me either, you didn't give me any choice.

Leonard Sirin and I . . .

Maud Isaac, his name is Isaac.

Leonard I will try to remember.

Maud That is the condition. Say it now – Isaac.

Leonard Isaac.

Maud Isaac, Isaac, Isaac.

Leonard I always hated the name.

Maud Never mind, say it again. Isaac.

Leonard I think I have got it.

Maud And keep reminding yourself, Isaac.

Leonard When shall I come?

Maud Next week sometime, I'll think about it and tell you.

Leonard Tomorrow.

Maud Impossible, his father will be here all day.

Leonard Not late afternoon, isn't he collecting a medal?

Maud You know more about us than us.

Leonard The town will be stopping for the ceremony.

Maud I forgot.

Leonard He will be gone a while.

Maud Alright, tomorrow, you can see him then.

Leonard I'll take him for a walk, or perhaps fishing.

Maud No, you will see him here.

Leonard With you standing over, poisoning his mind towards me.

Maud I won't interfere.

Leonard An hour alone with him.

Maud I'll do the washing. By the river. It takes half an hour.

Leonard I want to take him fishing.

Maud You must stay here with him. In this house. It is that or nothing.

Leonard You don't trust me.

Maud Not one bit.

He starts to go.

Leonard They won't grow, by the way. The soil is too sandy. Too thin, the water runs right through. You can't plant herbs here.

Maud It says on the packet –

Leonard They will say anything to sell you the seeds. Everyone knows that. You are so like my daughter in so many ways, but she would know that.

Maud Get out of here!

Leonard She would have known that from instinct.

Maud Get out!

Leonard It's strange. I thought all women knew that?

Maud Do I have to throw you out? Yell, and get the neighbours come running?

Pause.

Leonard It doesn't have to be like this, you and I want the same things.

Beat.

For the boy, I mean.

Beat.

Tomorrow then.

Maud In the evening.

Leonard I'll be here.

Maud Goodbye.

Leonard goes.

Maud looks at her plants.

She picks up a seed packet.

She tries to read it.

She throws it down.

SCENE FOUR

Grenville and Sirin by the river bank.

Sirin is sitting with a fishing rod. Grenville is adjusting it for him. He leans back in the sun.

Grenville The point isn't to catch fish anyway. That isn't why people come fishing. You'll understand that in time. They go fishing because it is what they do. Because it is a normal father-and-son thing to do, because they are seen to be normal if they do it. Because everyone thinks, ah yes, fathers and sons, that is what they do. Like kicking a football.

You never actually catch any fish. Or if you do, it's a bonus.

I've never seen a fish here, certainly not in winter, and I have practically lived in it for ten years. I've seen just about everything else. Things I wouldn't want you to see. Things I wouldn't ever want you to see.

It's funny, isn't it? Within days it just looks like a river again. But further upstream, where we were, you couldn't see the water for . . .

And on the other side, buildings. Already they are putting up new buildings. Isn't it funny how things change so quick?

He sits up.

34

Can you tell me something? I know you understand, but I want to know why you don't speak?

You can talk to me, you know. Only you don't have to. That is another father-and-son thing. We can understand each other without anything having to actually be said, if you want. Whatever you want.

Pause.

But the odd little word wouldn't go amiss.

There is tug on the line.

Now, what are you going to do? Isaac? You have got a tug on the line, better do something or it will get away.

Isaac doesn't do much.

Wheel it in, like I showed you.

Isaac starts to.

You are going to have to go faster than that.

Isaac goes faster.

That is the way, faster faster. Have you got it?

The fishing line appears. Nothing on it.

Never mind. There is always next time. I told you, we aren't here to catch fish anyway.

Isaac casts again.

You are good at that. How come you can do that without being shown? I would say you are excellent at that, I can't believe your mother has ever taught you. Do that again for me.

Isaac gets the line out and casts it again.

Very good indeed. Has someone else been taking you fishing?

Someone must have been taking you fishing.

Pause.

It's okay, I don't mind. After all, I wasn't around so I am glad that someone did.

Grenville leans back in the sun.

Someone may have started the process, but now I am here I will make sure you become a master.

Isaac continues to sit with the line.

SCENE FIVE

Outside the house. Grenville and Isaac.

Grenville might be carrying Isaac. They are both excited.

Mo? Mo! Mo!

He swings him around.

Mo? Mo, come out here.

Maud appears.

Maud Don't call me that.

Grenville Come here.

Maud What is it?

Grenville puts him down.

Grenville Do it again.

Maud Do what?

Grenville He spoke.

Maud No.

Grenville Say it again, Isaac.

Pause.

Maud He can't talk, Grenville, I told you.

Grenville He spoke I promise you, he said something to me.

Maud What?

Grenville I want him to say it. Isaac, say to your mother what you said to me.

Pause.

Isaac?

Maud You must have been imagining it.

Grenville No, now Isaac –

Maud Maybe it was a fluke.

Grenville I heard it.

He shakes him.

Maud Be gentle with him.

Grenville I am, I just –

Maud He's tired, perhaps he will talk later.

Grenville sits down with him.

Grenville He can speak, I know he can. Isaac? What is it? Why won't you say it now?

Maud He looks exhausted.

Grenville No.

Maud He's had a long day.

Grenville I have had a long day, I can still talk, can't I?

Maud He will talk later.

Maud takes him and hugs him.

37

Grenville You don't believe me?

Maud I didn't say that.

Grenville He will do it again.

Maud What did he say?

Pause.

Grenville He said fish.

Maud Fish?

Grenville We caught a fish, and he pointed to it straight away and said fish.

Maud You caught a fish?

Grenville It doesn't matter whether we caught a fish or not.

Maud I can make a pie.

Grenville The point isn't whether we caught a fish or not, the point is –

Maud I know the point.

Grenville I think maybe you are right, maybe you talk too much for him. From now on I think you should talk less around him.

Maud How can I do that?

Grenville We've got to listen to him.

Maud He will talk when he wants to talk.

Grenville But I think he wants to talk now.

Maud He is asleep now.

Grenville Later then. Before bed, we will try to get him to talk.

Maud Okay.

Grenville He said something else.

Maud Oh.

Grenville He said dada.

Maud Did he really?

Grenville I don't know why, we were just by the river.

Maud It is a universal first word.

Grenville I suppose it is.

Maud After mother.

Grenville He didn't say that.

Maud No.

Grenville coughs again.

Maud is concerned. She holds him while his body is racked with coughing.

Grenville Just the damp, we got damp sitting there.

Grenville takes his boots off.

I'll take him tomorrow.

Maud Where?

Grenville When I go to get my medals, I'll show him off.

Maud I would rather you didn't.

Grenville All the men, they would like to see.

Maud It might not be wise.

Grenville He is my son, isn't he?

Maud Of course he is, but the army – I don't want him to get any ideas.

Grenville What ideas? It's a state occasion.

Maud It isn't the place for a boy.

Grenville I want them to see him.

Maud I will bring him down later then, after the official stuff has been done. It will mean we don't have to stand around for as long.

Grenville You are sure you will come?

Maud Of course.

Pause.

Grenville You're right. Of course you are right. It would be too long a day for him anyway. It never crossed my mind. What would a boy want with a stuffy army ceremony? He would be bored out of his mind. You are so clever at these things.

Maud Thank you.

Grenville You don't need to thank me. It's you, you are the best the boy could want.

He leans back.

Grenville Who taught him to fish, by the way?

Beat.

He fishes well. You can't have taught him.

Maud Friends.

Grenville Friends.

Maud Friends' fathers.

Grenville I thought all the fathers were in the war.

Pause.

Anyway, it doesn't matter who. He can fish, that is good.
Every father wants a son who can fish.

Beat.

She strokes his hair.

Maud The two of you.

Grenville What?

Maud I love it.

Grenville Ow

Maud What is it?

Grenville I . . .

Maud Don't look into the sun.

Grenville Just then I . . .

Maud It doesn't look bright, but it tricks you.

Grenville It comes and goes this, it just starts, one minute
I am okay, the next . . .

Grenville sits up.

It is like there is lemon juice in my eye.

Maud You should never look at the winter sun.

Grenville It's not that, they water for no reason.

Maud Open them for me.

Grenville It hasn't been like this for a while.

Maud You've been in the outside all day.

Grenville Sometimes I can't see at all.

Maud When?

Grenville Broad daylight.

Maud It's the time of year, I told you.

Grenville No. I think I am going blind. Or I think I know what it must be like to be going blind. I can't see and it –

Pause.

– it is all just black.

Pause.

There is nothing but black. And in the black . . . whatever it is that is in the black, it's –

Maud I know.

Grenville Just there, chasing my tail, just right there behind me. Catching up. Faster faster, getting there. And the only thing you can do is open your eyes and see that it is nothing. It has gone. Gone. Until you close your eyes again.

But if you can't open your eyes, if they stay closed, or you can open your eyes but you can't see . . . then what?

She strokes his hair.

Maud You're shaking.

Grenville I'm going to go blind, aren't I?

Maud I don't know.

Grenville I don't want to go blind, Maud. Anything but blind.

Maud We will get you some treatment, see a doctor.

Grenville There is an ointment, I heard there might be an ointment.

Maud There you are then, we will get you the ointment.

Grenville It's expensive.

Maud We will get it. We will sell everything that we have if we have to, we will get it. We won't stop until we have it.

She kisses the top of his head.

Grenville Kiss my eyes.

She kisses them.

Maud Is that better?

She kisses them again.

You won't go blind. Don't worry. You won't go blind. I won't let you.

SCENE SIX

Sirin and Leonard by the table.

The herbs are in front of them.

Leonard is speaking. Sirin is saying nothing.

Leonard P is for parsley. Which is this one. Look here, a P, in chalk on the table.

He walks back up to the beginning and starts again.

And L for lemon grass.

He does the same thing.

Can you see the L? And M for marjoram

Leonard is watching him.

I will teach you your letters. I always meant to, and since they don't have you any toys. Sirin?

He sits down.

Why have you stopped, you say? You don't need to stop.

I have stopped because I have brought you something.
Oh Grandfather, what have you brought me, you say.

Leonard goes into his pocket.

He takes out a bag.

I brought you all I could afford.

Sirin takes the bag.

And you look in the bag, and you think, not bad, he
remembers that I have a sweet tooth, how could I forget
you have a sweet tooth, when I miss you as badly as I do?
all I can think about is your sweet tooth and consequently
I am running back and forwards to the sweet shop all day
long.

Sirin gives the bag back.

Aren't you going to eat them?

He offers them again.

Leonard puts them in Sirin's pocket.

Perhaps you will eat them later then. You can't have
grown out of your sweet tooth already? Hmm?

*Sirin takes them out of his pocket and puts them on
the table.*

Well, alright, I will eat them later then.
I still have a sweet tooth, as you know.

Leonard puts them into his pocket.

So what else have you been doing? That is what I say,
and you tell me you caught a fish. Well, I know that you
caught a fish because I saw you. And I say that I didn't
know that you could catch fish in the winter, and you say
that it was a special winter fish, and that you got to pull
its guts out and no doubt you ate it all for dinner with

her blessed parsley pie this is how it goes on so on and so forth, backward and forward. Conversation.

I miss you.

I miss you, Sirin, terribly.

Pause.

Leonard looks back into the sweet bag.

I'm just eating this so I don't cry. You are not supposed to see your grandfather cry, though of course you have seen your grandfather cry all the time. And you are not called Isaac. Never. Always remember you were Sirin first.

He takes a sweet out and puts in his mouth.

Anyway, sweets make you rot. And which is better out of rotting or crying is a moot point.

He puts them in his pocket.

What would you like to do?

Pause.

And you say you don't mind and I say we've got half an hour, and you say it is less than that by now, and I say we could play a game, and you say we could fight, and I ask you if you like fighting and you say that your father is a soldier, and I tell you that your father is dead, and you say no, he is collecting his medals, and I tell you that you must never ever call that man your father again. Do you hear?

There is a noise outside the door.

They both look around.

Leonard Can't the infernal woman even give us the full thirty minutes?

Maud walks in.

I've only just arrived.

Maud Too bad.

Leonard You said half an hour.

Maud I've left the clothes to soak.

Leonard You must have done it quick.

Maud I'll have to go back and get them so say goodbye.

Leonard We have hardly had time to say hello.

Maud He doesn't speak, it doesn't take him long.

Leonard He may not speak to you but that doesn't mean he doesn't speak.

Maud He is retarded, he can't speak.

Leonard That isn't true.

Maud If he could he would talk to me.

Leonard Maybe he doesn't want to. Sirin, say parsley.

Maud His name is Isaac.

Leonard Isaac, say parsley.

　Sirin says nothing.

Maud He is an imbecile.

Leonard Give him back, then.

Maud No.

Leonard You don't love him.

Maud That isn't true.

Leonard Not the way I do.

Maud More, I suspect.

Leonard You love him with some weird grief for another child, you don't love him for himself.

46

Maud Yesterday that might have been true, or the day before, but now –

You know the funny thing is that if you had asked for him back on the first day I might have been tempted. He wet the bed, he smashed the jug, he bit me as I tried to wash him. I thought, this is the worst child I have ever seen. I thought about hurting him, really hard, hitting or thumping him or anything just to relieve the frustration. But then the next morning, seeing him sleeping, or waking up and looking lost, or even the way he spooned in his breakfast, and rubbed his eye . . .

Leonard Spare me.

Maud He snuggled into my breast as if he had grown there.

Leonard How nice.

Maud You can't have him.

Leonard Then neither can you.

Maud Get out.

Leonard I need to see him again.

Maud No.

Leonard Every week, just one hour.

Maud I can't do that. You know I can't do that.

Leonard You will have to, you will have to find a way.

Maud I knew this would happen, I know men like you, give you an inch and you will take a mile. I never should have agreed to this.

Leonard You didn't have any choice.

   Pause.

I have remembered why you remind me of my daughter.

Maud Not this again.

Leonard You used to play with her.

Maud I don't think so.

Leonard Katharine. You and her were friends. Your sister and you used to come and play with her. When you were putting out the plants that first day, I saw a mark above your elbow.

Maud I don't have time for this.

Leonard Little twins, used to be so hard to tell you apart.

Maud You have to be joking.

Leonard Magda had the mark, Maud didn't.
  Even Katharine couldn't tell you apart otherwise.

Maud You mis-remember.

Leonard No, because Maud died with my daughter.
I remember pulling their bodies out of the water. And if you aren't Maud, you must be Magda.

Pause.

Maud Sirin, go and wait for your father.

He doesn't move.

Go and stand outside the door.

Sirin does nothing.

Move, I said.

Leonard Which must mean you are living in her shoes.

Sirin hangs on to her.

Maud Sirin?

She tries to carry him out.

48

He cries.

Leonard Tell me you aren't.
Tell me I am wrong.

Maud You are wrong.

Leonard I don't believe you.

Pause.

Grenville comes in.

He is in a good mood.

He takes his hat off.

Grenville Ah, we have company. I feel like celebrating.

He gets out a bottle of whisky from his pocket.

That is my last ever engagement from the army. That is
the last I ever have to see of the lot of them, and look –

He takes out a whole handful of medals.

– look Maud, medals and medals. We can hang them on
the mantelpiece. You can play with them, Isaac, put them
in your treasure box. We can use them as buttons if you
like. Would someone please smile at me. This is a
celebration.

Maud Well done

She kisses him.

Grenville A cold kiss?

She kisses him again, a little warmer.

Maud We have company.

Grenville I know, so why haven't we got him a glass
already? Have we met?

Maud He was just on his way out.

Grenville Well now he is on his way back in.

Maud He was going.

Grenville I insist he stays. Pleased to meet you . . .

Leonard Leonard.

Grenville A very good name. Maud, please, three glasses. Blow it, four, let's let Isaac have some whisky for a change.

Leonard I have been teaching the boy.

Grenville Good good, he needs to learn. What did you teach him?

Leonard His letters to begin with.

Grenville Don't tell me you taught him to fish. Maud, was this the man who taught him to fish?

Leonard Amongst other things.

Pause.

Grenville Well you did a good job.

Maud gets some glasses.

Grenville drinks.

Cheers.

They all drink.

So what else have you been teaching him?

Leonard The names of things, letters, things like that, how it is important not to mix one thing up for another.

Grenville Has he spoken to you?

Leonard Of course.

Grenville You see? You see, Maud, he spoke to him too. He doesn't speak to his mother, she thinks he can't.

Leonard He speaks very well.

Grenville Because he has an excellent teacher.

   The boy holds out his glass again.

   Grenville fills it up.

Maud No.

Grenville Why not, it isn't very often that his father gets decorated.

   Grenville drinks his as well.

We will both drink, eh?

   The boy drains it. So does Grenville.

A taste for it, eh?

   He fills it again.

Leonard I don't think –

Grenville Just once in a while.

Leonard I know, but he is just a boy.

Grenville He likes the taste.

Maud Leave it, Grenville.

Grenville Half a glass as a concession to his teacher.

   He carries on pouring.

A large half-glass.

Leonard He is just a child.

Grenville He is my boy, if he wants to drink he can.

   The boy and Grenville drink again.

   The boy puts his glass out again.

Leonard Sirin, no more.

Pause.

Put it down, Sirin.

Grenville looks at Leonard.

Grenville Sirin?

Maud His name is Isaac.

Grenville Why did he call him Sirin?

Leonard He shouldn't be drinking.

Grenville Why did you call him Sirin, when you know his name is Isaac?

Maud comes in between them.

Maud I have made some cordial, the boy can water his down with cordial.

She pours some.

Then we can all drink.

Grenville Will no one answer me?

Pause.

Maud He is an old man, he is confused.

Leonard I never felt younger.

Maud See he thinks he is young, well, clearly he is ancient.

Leonard My brain works as well as it ever did.

Maud More evidence of insanity.

Pause.

Leonard I would like a word alone with the soldier.

Pause.

Would that be alright?

Grenville You can talk here.

Leonard I would rather speak to you alone.

Grenville Maud?

Maud Don't listen to him.

Leonard Would you leave us?

Maud I don't want to go.

Grenville She doesn't want to go.

Leonard It would be better for her if she did.

Grenville But she doesn't want to, and I am not the sort of man to force a woman to do anything she doesn't want to do.

Pause.

Leonard Then another time.

Leonard stands up.

If she insists, I will speak to you another time. But I will speak to you. Thank you for the whisky. I am so glad about your medals.

Leonard goes round the table and kisses Sirin.

Grenville and Maud watch.

He leaves.

Maud takes a cloth and scrubs Sirin's face.

Grenville Where did he come from?

Maud I don't like him.

Grenville You have never mentioned him before.

Maud I didn't think it was important.

Grenville How do you know him?

Maud Not now.

Grenville Maud, answer me.

Maud Later. You put Isaac to bed. I have to go and collect the washing.

Maud picks up the washing basket.

Maud?

She leaves.

He rubs his eyes.

Maud?

Sirin gets up to leave as well. He knocks a chair over.

Isaac?

Sirin exits.

Grenville is left in the darkness of the blind.

Maud?

SCENE SEVEN

Late at night.

Maud by the river bank.

She wrings out the washing.

She looks out across the river.

She takes her shoes off and puts her feet in the water.

She sees something. She bends down to pick it up. She drags it out.

It is a soldier's hat.

She cleans it off.

There is a huge bullet-hole right through it.
She puts it back in the water.
She lets it float away.

SCENE EIGHT

The next morning. In the house.
Grenville is by the table. Maud comes in.

Maud I thought you'd be asleep.

Grenville No.

  Pause.

I have been up for hours, I have been out already.

Maud Oh.

Grenville You didn't come back last night.

Maud I didn't want to wake you up.

Grenville I waited for you.

Maud You shouldn't have done.

Grenville You said you were just getting the washing.

Maud I got delayed.

Grenville By what?

  Pause.

Maud The river, I was watching the river, I was looking for fish. I know that it is difficult to catch a fish in the winter but . . . you did, so I . . .

Grenville Bullshit. I feel like I don't know you any more.

Maud You have been away for ten years, it takes some time.

55

Grenville You aren't the same person.

Maud Of course not. Ten years, Grenville, I have changed, grown up for God's sake, had my thirtieth birthday.

Grenville It is not that.

Pause.

I had another attack last night. You weren't here. I needed you and you weren't here.

Pause.

Maud goes to the side and gets out a jar.

What is this?

Maud Ointment money.

She puts the jar in front of Grenville and puts the coins into it.

I found out about the ointment, and where you get it. When it is full, we'll be able to afford it.

Grenville How will we do that?

Maud The herbs are growing.

Grenville The soil is too barren.

Maud Maybe, but look. Little leaves coming. This one has a flower.
And when they have grown, we will sell them, and then the ointment.

Grenville I saw the teacher. I just came back just now. I had breakfast with the teacher. He lives just a mile away. He says we should call the boy Sirin.

Pause.

56

And I am happy for that. I never liked the name Isaac anyway, if you must know. Sirin suits him better. Don't you think?

Maud It is up to you.

Grenville Your opinion is important.

Maud I prefer Isaac.

Pause.

Grenville Sirin it is.

Pause.

He said I should call you Magda. Not Maud, but Magda.

Beat.

Grenville Why would he say that?

Maud He is mad, I told you before.

Grenville No.
He seemed quite lucid to me. The things he told me, it seemed that I was going mad. Or you were mad, or perhaps both. He told me . . .

Pause.

Grenville He told me that Maud died. I am sorry I . . . And Isaac died with her.
Now why would he say that?

Maud How can I have died, I am right here?

Grenville He said –

Maud A mistake, Magda died, yes, I should know, I mourned her, but Maud, no . . .

Grenville The mark above your arm –

Maud We both had it.

Grenville Maud didn't. No, that is the thing, see . . .

I remember she didn't. The night we first made love, she showed me her arm with no mark on it, not a blemish, and said this was the only difference between the two. Maud didn't have it. That is the funny thing. She didn't.

He sits down.

Pause.

So what should I do?

Pause.

We will call him Isaac if you prefer. Whatever you want. Or Sirin, as I want. I don't care, but . . .

Pause.

I would rather you didn't wear my ring. That is the only thing I will ask. Everything else, as you want. But my ring . . .

Maud looks at her hand.

Take my ring off.

Pause.

It wasn't meant for you. It was meant for her.

Maud tries.

Here –

He pulls on her finger.

Am I hurting you?

He pulls again.

Why aren't you saying if I am hurting you?

The ring comes off. It has hurt her.

He goes to the fireplace and searches in the ashes.

Maud It isn't there.

Grenville Where is it?

Maud I threw it in the river as you asked.

Grenville Then you will wear no ring.

Maud As you want.

Grenville I want.

Grenville comes and sits back at the table.

They are building a new city across the river. Did you know that?
The first storey already.

Maud Oh.

Grenville You can see it from this bank. There are supposed to be jobs, Mo.

Maud Please don't call me that.

Grenville What did you say?

Maud Please don't call me that.

Pause.

Grenville I don't know what to call you.

Sirin comes in from upstairs.

Maud goes over to him. They embrace.

She picks him up and carries him to the table.

You don't have to lift him like that, he isn't a baby.

She puts him down.

He can walk, can't he?

Maud Of course he can.

Grenville Then let him walk.

Sirin walks.

Maud gets a chair for him.

You don't need to do that, he can get his own chair. Leave the chair, woman. Sirin, get your own chair –

Sirin pulls the chair out.

– and your own breakfast. You can get your own breakfast perfectly well. I don't like the way you have her running about after you. From now on you will do things for yourself a little more.

Maud He doesn't know where things are kept.

Grenville Then he can find out. Sirin, go to the cupboard and get out your own bowl.

Sirin doesn't move.

Stand up and go to the cupboard.

Sirin stands up.

Walk to the cupboard, and get out your own bowl.

Sirin opens the cupboard.

Maud He can't reach.

Grenville Then he will have to grow.

Maud reaches up for a bowl for him.

Put it back.

Maud He needs his breakfast.

Grenville He won't starve. He can learn to look after himself. I told you.

Maud puts it back.

If he can't reach the bowl he can eat off the table. Maud, pour him his porridge on the table.

Maud does nothing

Pour his porridge on the table, I said.

Maud pours the porridge on the table.

Sirin sits down.

And now you can eat it.

Sirin eats it with his hands.

Not like that, with a spoon, you imbecile.

Grenville hits him.

Sirin cries.

Get yourself a spoon.

Sirin cries again.

A spoon, I said.

He hits him again.

He doesn't even know where the spoons are kept. Maud, what have you been teaching this child? Well if he doesn't know where the spoons are, there is no point in his having breakfast. No breakfast today, Isaac. Go and clean yourself up.

Sirin looks at him.

He hits him again. Hard.

Go and clean yourself up.

Sirin goes to the sink.

Leave him Maud, he has to learn.

Maud makes a move towards Sirin, Grenville grabs her arm and stops her.

You mustn't be soft on him.

Sirin is snivelling.

Grenville pushes him. Hard.

Clean up, I said.

Sirin does nothing. Another push. Sirin falls to the floor.

Clean up. Can't you hear me?

Grenville kicks the child, who curls up on the floor. Once twice. Three times.

Sirin cries out. Maud tries to intervene again, but Grenville grabs her and pushes her, roughly.

I won't have you being soft on him either.

Grenville stands up.

I have to go into town. I don't know how long I will be.
The teacher is coming this morning for his lesson as always. I said you would be here and would welcome him. No arguments, it is good for the boy to learn. There are lots of things this boy has to learn. And if he doesn't learn you will have to learn to beat him too. Hard, until he breaks. We will both have to learn to beat him.

Grenville walks out.

Maud picks up Sirin and comforts him.

Maud Shush shush, there you go. You are okay now. Hey little one, you are okay.

She rocks him.

I'll make you some breakfast. He has gone now. It's okay, my love.

Leonard is outside his house. He is planting some shrubs.

Maud and Sirin arrive.

She is carrying Sirin on her hip.

She watches him.

Maud So he hit you too.

  Leonard turns round.

Leonard Just a bruise, nothing.

Maud It looks more than that.

Leonard I was just coming to you.

Maud Why did you tell him?

Leonard He threatened me.

Maud We could have kept it going, but now . . .

Leonard You weren't going to let me see the boy, were you?

  Sirin cries.

Maud It's okay.

Leonard What has happened to him?

Maud He is okay.

Leonard He is frightened.

Maud He will be alright. His father has a temper, you know that.

  Maud puts him down.

  Sirin hangs on to her.

Go to your grandfather.

Sirin won't move.

It is your grandfather, go to him.

Leonard Here, Sirin?

Sirin hangs on to her.

Maud You will have to take him.

Leonard I thought you wanted him.

Maud I can't keep him, not now.

Leonard You mean he should come here?

Maud Grenville has turned back into a soldier. He will kill him before long, this morning I saw it, just a little hit but now he knows he isn't his . . .

Leonard I can't take him.

Maud He is your grandchild.

Leonard But you said yourself, I am getting old. You know I can't.

Maud You said you wanted him.

Leonard When you had him, I wanted him, but now –

Maud Grenville will kill him.

Leonard You will have to find somewhere else for him.

Maud He is your grandchild.

Leonard It doesn't count for anything.

Pause.

I can't manage, and anyway, for how long? I am finding it more and more difficult to look after myself, but with a child.

Maud What about for your daughter's sake?

Leonard Katharine.

Maud Katharine.

Leonard Don't say it as if you don't know her name.

Maud What about for Katharine?

Leonard She didn't love him any more than I did. She was always wishing him on someone else. She tried to lose him when she was pregnant, she twisted her ankle trying to abort, and when he was born he was such a strange child, it was the same. The silence, it drives you mad. You have to have both sides of the conversation to yourself. No one can live with that.

Maud He will learn.

Leonard He won't learn. He is eight already. He should have learnt by now.

Maud He said fish.

Leonard No.

Maud Grenville said he said fish.

Leonard You didn't even hear it yourself? The number of times I have thought I heard him say something, one word maybe in amongst the silence, but even if he did, what is one word when he needs a dictionary to be able to talk? Conversation, Maud, is made of more than one word. Fish, he says, oh, you say, fish, he says again, ah, you say, fish from him a third time, it doesn't add up to much, does it? He is an imbecile, face it.

Pause.

A little bruising from his father won't harm him. Like it won't harm me. You can continue to bring him here for his lessons, if you need a break. Once a week for an hour or so. I would like that.

Maud I can't live that way.

Leonard Then you will have to find another way by yourself.

Maud looks at his plants.

Maud How come your plants do so well? The soil is the same, and yet yours are twice the size.

Leonard I add chalk. The soil is too full of sand. It doesn't hold the water, the plants dry out. So I add a little chalk.

Maud nods.

Maud Where do you get the chalk from?

Leonard It is dangerous. Lime, you have to dig it with your hands.

Maud Could you get me some?

Leonard You have to be careful, if you add it to water it corrodes. Skin, flesh, bone, whatever comes in its path. I knew a man who dropped a little on his hand, then with the rain, a hole straight through.

Maud The marjoram would benefit, you say.

Leonard Just a little, under the surface. To counteract the sand.

Maud Would you get me some? I think the herbs could do with some.

Leonard Of course.

Pause.

You will learn the way of the plants. You are clever, you will soon get the hang of it.

And the boy, you will soon learn the way of him. Even the father. You'll soon get the way. Plenty have before you. You'll manage.

Grenville by the river.

He takes his boots off.

He gets out his fishing line.

He can't see any more.

Grenville Just because I can't see you, doesn't mean I won't catch you.

He rubs his eyes.

Just because I . . . I can sense that you are there. And I am right behind you. I am on your tail. I will get you, little fishes, don't worry.

He rubs his eyes again.

No, not here.

He rubs them again.

Stop. Stop, I said, I know you aren't there. There is nothing there, you black. STOP, STOP.

The pedlar comes and sits down next to him.

Who is that?

Grenville turns round.

Trent Your line isn't out.

Grenville I know.

Trent You won't catch anything that way.

Grenville I can see.

Trent I just thought you might like . . .

Grenville No thank you.

Grenville re-casts.

Trent You've all got it, haven't you?

Pause.

This parasite. A whole generation of blind soldiers.

Grenville I am not blind.

Trent Not yet.

Trent looks across the river to the other side.

That is going to be one of my houses over there. I don't know if you can see it, but one of the new ones. First storey going up already. You see the staircase. Just up to the landing. Got my name down and everything.

It's a good job that all you soldiers have gone blind, because, whatever happens, the war can't start again, can it?

He chuckles.

The war can't start because who the hell would they fight with?

Grenville grabs the pedlar and holds his throat.

Trent Get off.

Grenville Who are you anyway?

Trent Just a pedlar.

Grenville I am not going blind.

Trent I didn't say.

Grenville I am not going blind.

Trent Listen, mister, you are hurting me.

Grenville throttles him more.

Eventually he stops.

The pedlar draws breath, obviously really hurt.

He gets up.

Grenville is sitting up.

The pedlar kicks him. Once, twice.

Grenville does nothing.

The pedlar leaves.

Grenville cries.

SCENE ELEVEN

Back at the house.

Maud has laid the table. There is a cloth, and on it flowers.

She has laid the table for two.

She might even light a candle.

Grenville comes in.

He opens the door.

He has a little difficulty walking to the table.

Maud notices and takes his hand. She leads him to the table.

She pulls out a chair.

Grenville Thanks.

She kisses the top of his head.

I tried to catch a fish.

Maud It is very hard to catch a fish in winter.

Pause.

She puts a plate of food down in front of him.

Grenville What is it?

Maud Vegetables.

Grenville Oh.

Maud Parsnips and carrots.

Grenville Where is Isaac?

Maud Asleep. I put him to bed early.

Grenville I am going to teach him to talk. I decided.

Maud Of course.

Grenville If others can talk then so can he.

Pause.

Grenville looks down at the plate.

I can't see it, Maud. Carrots and parsnips. That should be orange and white, shouldn't it, all I see is grey.

Maud The light isn't very good.

Grenville It isn't the light, and after the grey comes black.

Pause.

Maud I got you something today.

Grenville Oh.

Maud Some ointment. I've made it up already.

Grenville Where did you get it from?

Maud I sold all the plants. The apples from the back. I sold just about everything that we had.

Grenville Did you see a doctor?

Maud Of course.

She gets out a little plate of white stuff.

He said you will be right as rain.

She takes it over to him.

He said it will sooth the eyes, get rid of the infection.
It can all be reversed.

Grenville Let me feel.

He puts his fingers into it.

Maud Doesn't that feel nice?

Grenville What did the doctor look like?

Maud Old and kindly. He said it was the same with all
the soldiers.

Grenville His voice?

Maud Soothing. He had seen it all before.

Grenville Was he a good doctor?

Maud Of course he was.

Grenville Put it on for me.

She stands behind him.

She puts it on with her fingers.

Maud There we are. How does it feel?

Grenville Cold.

Maud Don't shut them, keep them open if you can.

Grenville Will it sting?

Maud Only a little.

She carries on putting it on him.

I may be Magda, Grenville, and not Maud, but it doesn't mean that I don't love you. I always loved you, you know that. Even when I was a kid I loved you, and then when we were teenagers, and all you could see was Maud, I was still loving you. Fiercer even. The more you and she became inseparable the more I wanted . . . Standing on the sidelines trying to say, love Magda, love Magda. But it was always Maud. Maud Maud Maud.

Grenville Don't . . .

Maud I wish I had been Maud, Grenville. That is all. My whole life I wish I had been Maud. And if I could be, I would.

   Pause.

How does it feel now?

Grenville Hot.

Maud That is all. We've nearly finished it now.

Grenville It isn't ointment, is it?

   Pause.

It is stinging, Maud. You must feel that on your fingers. The tears in my eyes, they are making it worse. What are you waiting for? If it is lime, it needs water. Simple chemistry tells you that. If it is to eat through my skull you must add water. There is water on the table, I am sure you took the precaution of that. Throw a glass of water in my face, Maud, and it will be over.

   Maud picks up the glass.

Don't hesitate now. What? At the final hurdle, you hesitate? Maud wouldn't have. If she had planned to do something she . . .

Maud throws the glass of water in his face.

The water reacts with the lime. Steam comes off.

Grenville screams.

She holds him while he screams.

Maud It's okay, it's okay.
Shush. It is okay.

SCENE TWELVE

Trent sitting by the river bank.

He takes his boots off. He looks over to the other bank. He sees something.

Trent Oi. Why is there no one working today? It's not a Sunday. Where has everyone gone. You've only got half way up to the first landing. I need a second storey on my house if I am to live there. Hey?
Where is everyone? Why has the work stopped?

He picks up a stone and throws it over to the other bank.

Is there no one there?
What about my house?

He picks up another stone and throws it.

What about my house? You can't just stop now?

SCENE THIRTEEN

Maud and Sirin outside.

They are playing on a rug.

Sirin Fish.

Maud Fish and fish and fish, my love.

Sirin Fish fish fish fish.

Maud You say it loud.

Sirin Fish.

Maud laughs.

Fish.

She laughs again.

Maud Who said you can't have a conversation with a single word?

Sirin Fish fish fish.

Leonard comes in.

Maud Look, we are talking. He says fish and then I say fish and then he says fish and on and on, until we have discussed the cares of the world and philosophy and told each other long rambling stories about epic tales and laughed at complex and subtle jokes. You wouldn't believe the jokes he can tell. The punchlines he can dream up with a single word. Tell your jokes now, Sirin. Well, he is shy now, but the jokes . . .

Leonard sits down.

You would laugh at the jokes, I know you would.

Leonard Your plants?

Maud Flourishing

Leonard It did the trick?

Maud You knew it would.
    You?

Leonard All healed.

Maud Good.

Pause.

The best one is this one he tells about this man who –

Leonard I have just come from the town

Pause.

Maud Anyway the man, he doesn't know whether he –

Leonard The war is starting again.

Pause.

That is what they are saying.

Maud It's a joke.

Leonard No joke.

Maud A rumour then, the war is over.

Leonard I thought it was a rumour, so I went up to a town official and asked him, is it a rumour, I asked.

Maud He said of course it is.

Leonard He said he wished it were. There were tears in his eyes. It's a new war, he said.

Pause.

You talk about jokes, well, he told me one. And he wasn't a funny man. But this one, a funny thing. How can it be? I said to him, this new war, how can we go to war? What do you mean, he said to me, we can go to war as easily as we can clap our hands. It wasn't the answer I expected so I went on. But the soldiers, I said. What about the soldiers, he said. The soldiers are all sick, they have this parasite. The soldiers, he asked. Yes, the soldiers I said.

And do you know what he said to me then?

This next war won't need soldiers.

Pause.

75

That is the punchline, by the way. This next war won't need soldiers. I laughed at that, he was serious. How can there be a war without soldiers? I said. He didn't answer.

Pause.

It's impossible, isn't it? Like a self-defeating . . .
HOW CAN THERE BE A WAR WITHOUT SOLDIERS? I said.

Pause.

Maud We have been sitting in the sun, and . . .

Leonard How can there be?

Pause.

Maud In this house, whatever happens out there, in this house . . .

Leonard Maud?

Maud Peacetime. That is all I know.

Pause.

It's peacetime here, you understand. There is no more of this, not here. Not just as Sirin is learning to talk. No, not now. We are in a different land to out there. They're in one season, but we are in another. You understand? In the four walls of the garden –

Leonard I don't even understand it.

Maud So don't mention it. It's gone. You didn't go into the town today, you won't again. They might have rumours over there, they might not. It doesn't affect us, does it? What we are is what we are here. That's all. Nothing more. Three souls and a house.
And a sky and a sun.
A garden.

The plants will grow or not. Sirin will talk or not. We will eat or not. That is it. It's over, do you understand me? There is no war.

Leonard Even as . . . ?

Maud Peacetime.

Leonard looks at the sky.

Leonard The sun.

Maud And the four walls of the house. That's all.

Leonard Peacetime then.

Sirin claps.

Maud claps back.

Maud Peacetime.